THE
VOLUNTEER
Survival Guide

Books by Jason Young and Jonathan Malm

The Come Back Effect
The Volunteer Effect
The Volunteer Survival Guide

THE VOLUNTEER
Survival Guide

Your Question-and-Answer
Resource for Volunteering

Jason Young AND Jonathan Malm

BakerBooks
a division of Baker Publishing Group
Grand Rapids, Michigan

Published by Baker Books
a division of Baker Publishing Group
PO Box 6287, Grand Rapids, MI 49516-6287
www.bakerbooks.com

Printed in the United States of America

Library of Congress Cataloging-in-Publication Data
Names: Young, Jason, 1978– author. | Malm, Jonathan, author.
Title: The volunteer survival guide : your question-and-answer resource for
    volunteering / Jason Young and Jonathan Malm.
Description: Grand Rapids, Michigan : Baker Books, a division of Baker Publishing
    Group, 2020.
Identifiers: LCCN 2020023159 | ISBN 9781540901064
Subjects: LCSH: Voluntarism—Religious aspects—Christianity. | Lay ministry.
Classification: LCC BR115.V64 Y685 2020 | DDC 253/.7—dc23
LC record available at https://lccn.loc.gov/2020023159

The authors are represented by the literary agency of The Blythe Daniel Agency, Inc.

20 21 22 23 24 25 26   7 6 5 4 3 2 1

Contents

1

What Does It Take to Be a Great Volunteer?

STORY: **Jonathan**

Dennis was one of the first people I met while volunteering with the welcome team at my church.

He had a great smile, high-fived everyone he saw, and made people feel like they were walking into a party thrown just for them. I remember thinking, *I'd like to be more like Dennis in my role here.*

I assumed he'd been on staff at a church before or, at the very least, been volunteering with the welcome team for years. As I got to know him, though, I realized that wasn't the case. He worked in the Air Force doing cybersecurity. And he hadn't been on the team that long—only five months, about as long as I had.

The fact that he was such an amazing volunteer confused me a bit. Technically, I'm the expert. I've written books about volunteers and welcome teams and church stuff, yet he was better than me. He was so enthusiastic and happy, and he made everyone who walked into the room feel special. It felt like he had been waiting for you to show up all morning—even if you'd never met him before.

Between services one Sunday, I told him, "You're incredible, Dennis. How are you such a great volunteer? It seems like you're always here."

His normally bright smile slid off his face, and he got serious. "Church has been a bit of an oasis for me, to be honest. I'm going through a really rough breakup, and my ex-girlfriend's making trouble for me at work. I don't like to think about what I'd be doing if I wasn't here at church all day. So I make it a priority to be here. It's kind of like therapy for me, really."

We talked a bit more about the details of the situation—I didn't want to rush through his story—but I was still curious about his role. So when I felt like it was appropriate to bring it up again, I said, "But why are you here all the time? Do our leaders just schedule you every week? Do you make yourself available for that?"

"Oh, I've never been scheduled," he said. "Is that how they do it?"

"Hold on a second!" I said. "You aren't even officially on the team?"

"Nope."

"But you have the volunteer badge and everything. Did you just ask someone where they were one day and put one on?"

"Pretty much," Dennis said. "I saw people high-fiving guests in the front and I thought, 'I can do that.' So I asked someone where the badges were and started doing it."

My jaw dropped. I was so surprised by his answer, I didn't even know how to respond.

Eventually, I realized we should probably get him on the official team. I called my team leader over and introduced him to Dennis.

That interaction made me analyze why Dennis was such a great volunteer. I don't know if he even realized how good he was—it was just instinct for him. But I realized I wanted to be more like him. I wanted to be a great volunteer.

○ ○ ○

What we know about you is that you want to be a great volunteer. Nobody gets into a new role—whether volunteer or paid—to be mediocre. You want to feel like you bring something significant to your team.

We all get into volunteering for different reasons. Do you see yourself wanting to do one of these?

- *Make friends.* You're new at church and want to get connected.
- *Have fun.* You see those social media posts of people laughing and hanging out while serving, and you want to be part of that.

- *Serve God.* You want to be part of something bigger than yourself. God's done so much for you; you want to do something for him.
- *Make a difference.* There's a need at church, and you have the talent or resources to meet it.
- *Develop your skills.* You dabble in photography and want to get better. It's part practice, part learning from the rest of the team members.
- *Stay in the atmosphere.* You're like Dennis, and you want to be at church whenever the doors are open. Volunteering is a way you can do that.

Those are all great reasons to volunteer, and your story is probably a combination of a few of them.

That's one of the beautiful things about churches. We all come from different backgrounds, personalities, and motivations. But we're all part of the church, the greatest thing Jesus ever built on this earth. We all want to see the church succeed.

So what does it take to be a great volunteer? Jesus gave us a model. His disciples were squabbling about who would be the greatest among them. The story goes like this:

> Jesus called them together and said, "You know that the rulers of the Gentiles lord it over them, and their high officials exercise authority over them. Not so with you. Instead, whoever wants to become great among you must be your servant, and whoever wants to be first must be your slave—just as the Son of Man did not come to be served, but to serve,

and to give his life as a ransom for many." (Matt. 20:25–28 NIV)

Jesus made it clear that it wasn't a title that would make us great. It wasn't power to tell people what to do. It was serving. Serving others makes us great.

Now, you've already joined the volunteer team. You're already serving others. So according to Jesus, you're already becoming great. But we believe there are five specific elements that make you great at serving on a volunteer team.

Grateful

> Let every detail in your lives—words, actions, whatever—be done in the name of the Master, Jesus, thanking God the Father every step of the way. (Col. 3:17 Message)

Being a great volunteer starts with a sense of gratitude. You get to be a representative of Jesus. What an honor! Whether that's changing diapers, clicking buttons, parking cars, taking pictures, or shaking hands, you're helping build the church. Think of the Boeing employee who uses the tray table they helped assemble. Or the Apple employee who designed that button on the right side of iPhones. It might be a small contribution, but they can be grateful and proud that they got to be part of it. They might even point it out to their kids: "See this? I got to help build it."

We want to encourage you to volunteer as a representative of Jesus and be thankful for the opportunity. It's a privilege to serve God. Remember that being great is all about serving others.

Responsive

> Do nothing from selfish ambition or conceit, but in humility count others more significant than yourselves. Let each of you look not only to his own interests, but also to the interests of others. (Phil. 2:3–4)

One of the greatest gifts you can give your volunteer leader is to be responsive to their communication. If they schedule you to serve, let them know quickly whether or not you'll be there. While "no" feels like a negative word, they would rather hear that than wonder whether or not you'll be there when you're scheduled. Remember, your volunteer leader is dealing with many different pieces each week. They might not remember that you'd scheduled a vacation. They more often see a bunch of blank spaces on a page they need to fill. So be quick to communicate with both your leaders and fellow volunteers. This will also help keep assumptions from coming into the mix, which can taint relationships.

Enthusiastic

> Rejoice in the Lord always. I will say it again: Rejoice! (Phil. 4:4 NIV)

The funny thing about rejoicing is that you can't do it while looking bored. It takes energy. It takes enthusiasm.

The apostle Paul tells us to rejoice always. That includes when you're serving as a volunteer. Bring energy and enthusiasm to your role.

We aren't saying you need to be loud and obnoxious with nervous energy. Enthusiasm needs to match the setting. Whether you're outgoing or more reserved, you can bring enthusiasm to your role. It could be a smile, a tone of voice, kindness . . . Small moments make up enthusiasm in your role.

All In

> To those who use well what they are given, even more will be given, and they will have an abundance. But from those who do nothing, even what little they have will be taken away. (Matt. 25:29 NLT)

Own your role. Own your talents. Remember that God has given you this opportunity to serve him in your capacity as a volunteer. He's also given you talents to help you fulfill that mission. You can walk with confidence and a sense of ownership. If you see something that needs to be done, don't just wait for your leader to ask you to do it. Pitch in and help.

The beautiful thing about the economy of God is that he gives us even more when we take responsible ownership of the things he's entrusted to us. Your team needs you fully present, all in, with your head in the game.

Teachable

> Give instruction to a wise man, and he will be still wiser;
> teach a righteous man, and he will increase in
> learning. (Prov. 9:9)

It's not what you know that makes you a great volunteer; it's what you're willing to learn. Learn what your leader's heart is for your team. Learn how to be better in your role on the team. Seek knowledge. And be humble when it comes to feedback.

Remember Dennis? He had all of these great assets, and he was especially good at being teachable. The irony about us (Jason and Jonathan) is that sometimes our knowledge keeps us from being the best volunteers. Since we're "experts" at church, we sometimes aren't the most teachable people. The truth is we both have a lot to learn from people like Dennis. We'll never get to a place where we don't have more to learn.

Being teachable can take you places expertise never will.

○ ○ ○

In your journey to become a great volunteer, let this become your prayer:

God, I pray I will always be grateful for the opportunity you've given me to use my time and talents for you. I don't want to ever take it for granted or go about my role half-heartedly. I want to give it my all. Lord, remind me I'm a steward of this team I'm on. Give me a sense of ownership to take responsibility for what I can do. More than anything, I pray you would teach me. Teach me to love my leaders, to learn what excellence means, and to learn from correction. Jesus, give me humility like you modeled. Make me a servant.

2

How Can You Be the Ultimate Team Player?

STORY: **Jason**

Monique was looking to be part of something meaningful. She was a teacher, but she wanted to volunteer at church. She joined the greeter team.

A few months after joining the team, I noticed there was something different about her. Actually, there was something different about the team, and I traced it back to her. The whole team was getting better because she was there.

- Everyone on the team was showing up for their position more consistently.
- The greeters did their job with more enthusiasm.

- The vibe of the team began to feel even more like a community.

It felt like she was a team leader without having that title. She was serious about what she was doing on the team, and that burden spread to other volunteers. Not only that, but her care went beyond just Sunday mornings. She checked in on people and developed relationships with other team members.

Monique didn't do any of these things to be noticed. She just knew what type of team she wanted to be on, and she did her part to make it that way.

And I did notice. I soon asked her to be one of our leaders and even to be part of an internship during the summer while she wasn't teaching. I've seen her take her team to an even greater level in this leadership role. But I also loved seeing how much of an impact she could make by simply being the ultimate team player on our team.

○ ○ ○

We've all seen the power that can come from a great team. Even a football team with mediocre players can become great by learning to work together. And then if you put a few stars in the mix who learn how to work with their team members, you get championships. Teamwork is vital to sports.

It's also vital to baking. When the right ingredients come together, their mixture can produce something greater than the individual pieces. Simple oil, flour, water, and yeast can turn into a delicious piece of bread. All of those ingredients, crafted together and applied to the right process, create something great.

If you want to be part of a great team, it's important to bring the right ingredients to the table. The beautiful thing is that this is something you can do. You don't have to wait for others to do it. You can become the ultimate team player and make your team better by being involved.

There are four main actions—main ingredients—we see that make up an ultimate team player.

Assuming the Best

> Love never gives up, never loses faith, is always hopeful, and endures through every circumstance. (1 Cor. 13:7 NLT)

No matter how good a team is, it will always be imperfect, because people are imperfect. People will make mistakes and say or do things we don't understand. It's easy to question motives and make negative assumptions. *Why did they do that? Why did they say that? They must think . . .* If we let those types of assumptions grow, they can fracture the team dynamic. It becomes you versus them.

But when we believe others want to do their best and want to work as a team, we're able to overlook little things. We assume the best about others' motives, and it keeps us together. Then we can celebrate wins and losses as a team. "We succeeded" or "we made a mistake" keeps us working together and sharing the load. That all starts by assuming the best. It's the oil that keeps us operating smoothly while we're in close proximity.

Being a Friend

> The sweet smell of incense
>> can make you feel good,
>> but true friendship
>> is better still. (Prov. 27:9 CEV)

You trust your teammates. You value them. But do you like them? Are you friends with them?

Partners can accomplish much, but friends can accomplish even more. Partners tend to do their part of the deal and no more, while friends will go above and beyond to do more than what's required. When we like one another, we help and support instead of just tolerate one another.

The easiest way to be a friend to those on your team is to listen, remember, and ask. Listen to what's going on in their lives. Remember those details. Then ask about developments. Find common ground and genuinely care about those on your team. Be the glue that holds your teammates together.

Learning from and Teaching Others

> Now teach these truths to other trustworthy people who will
> be able to pass them on to others. (2 Tim. 2:2 NLT)

In business, there's a concept called *trade secrets*. It's the way a company does specific things that helps them operate better than their competitors. Formulas, processes, information—companies guard those secrets closely so they don't lose their edge.

In ministry, though, trade secrets shouldn't exist. We should all learn from and teach each other.

Your team should never fall apart because you unexpectedly got sick. Teach others your processes so they can cover for you. Then learn their processes so you can cover for them. Everyone and everything gets better when we grow and learn together.

Encouraging Others

Therefore encourage one another and build one another up, just as you are doing. (1 Thess. 5:11)

Look for opportunities to encourage your fellow teammates. Spread positivity.

Believe it or not, one of the best things you can do as a volunteer is not necessarily the task that you were assigned. Parking cars, watching kids, handing out bulletins—those are important roles and should be done with excellence. But the way you encourage your team members and maintain a positive attitude while doing it can make everyone better. Then it's no longer you doing the task but the whole team moving forward with a common purpose. You have the opportunity to lift up the whole team with your demeanor and words.

○ ○ ○

Just like Monique was a leader on her team long before she had a title, you can lead your team. If you're the one bringing the right ingredients to the table, people will naturally look to you as a leader. The ultimate team player sees their responsibility to lead others and makes everyone better for it.

This week, we encourage you to pick one of the four main ingredients and bring them to your team's table. Assume the best. Befriend someone who seems to be on the periphery of the group. Teach someone what you do and learn what they do. Find a chance to encourage someone who seems discouraged. Pick one thing, do it, and see what that small change can do for your group. Then do another thing next week. In a short time, can you imagine what your team would start looking like?

Here's a prayer to get you started on this journey:

God, teach me how to be a team player. I know you have placed me on my team for a purpose, and I want to give them my best. Remind me that it is not about me but about us.

3

What Do You Uniquely Bring to the Table?

STORY: **Jonathan**

Jessica co-leads the VIP team with me. We're the team that helps newcomers feel like insiders—from disconnected to connected.

It's funny, though, because we're almost completely opposite when it comes to personality and function on the team. Where I'm the outgoing, ultra-extrovert, she's the one who enjoys systems and behind-the-scenes tasks. Sure, she stands in our VIP room and welcomes people, but she's much happier scheduling people and operating our systems.

I'm grateful for Jessica, because I'm horrible with systems. If it were up to me, I'd be standing in the VIP room by myself for every service, trying to welcome the ten to twenty first-time guests each Sunday. I would forget to organize other volunteers to help me out.

And forget about any follow-up during the week. Where Jessica makes sure each newcomer gets a text as well as a listening ear, I'd drop the ball. I'd have the best intentions to reach out to first-time guests, but one small distraction would derail those intentions.

At the same time, Jessica values what I bring to the table, because I'm unashamed to meet anyone. I love going out in the line between services and greeting everyone. I love hyping up my teammates to welcome our guests. Jessica's the steady, the constant, and I'm the excitement. The team works because we understand what makes each of us unique, and we operate within that individuality.

○ ○ ○

There are some things, such as what we talked about in the first two chapters, that every team needs from every team member. Teamwork and excellence are things every single one of us should bring to the table.

But there are things inside you right now that we can't even predict. Your skills and aptitudes will be unique assets to your team. You have something that makes you unique to the team, and it's a wonderful thing when you learn what that is and then give it back to your church.

Did you know the brain is split up into different parts? Each part has a different function:

- the frontal lobe: problem solving, speech, intelligence
- the parietal lobe: sense of touch, language interpretation

- the occipital lobe: vision
- the temporal lobe: memory, hearing

These sections of the brain act almost like special agents. They have specific functions that they do better than any other part of the brain. And our bodies function best when they operate consistently with how they were made.

That's how we all are. We're designed by God to function best a certain way. Call it personality, aptitude, motivational gifts . . . We all have a unique function. Do you know what yours is?

You might find yourself in one of the following categories.

Problem Solver and Activity Coordinator

You aren't into sitting around too long. You certainly aren't into waiting. You see the problem, take responsibility, and work toward solving it. That means you're great at directing people to no-nonsense solutions.

If this is you, you're great at high-pressure situations. You can direct traffic, solve problems on the fly, and speed up processes. Every team needs someone like this. At the same time, you have to realize not everyone on your team may be like this. A little bit of patience and care with your words can go a long way.

This personality type is Jason, by the way.

Encourager and Atmosphere Setter

You love working with people. Whether that's collaboration, persuading others, or just opening up to them, your life is oriented around people. You love encouraging them and changing their bad days into good days.

If this is you, you're great at roles that involve motivating people. You can make them feel welcomed, make them smile, and help set an atmosphere of fun at your church. At the same time, your intensity can be overwhelming to some, and you can sometimes have an unhealthy desire for attention. It's important to remember there are times to be silent and get down to work.

This is Jonathan, by the way.

Detail Lover and Small-Task Obsessor

You love calmly approaching tasks. If you start something, you'll finish it, and you'll make sure your t's are crossed and your i's are dotted. You're extremely dependable, and you love supporting a vision by thinking through all the details.

If this is you, you're great at roles that require consistency and details. You'll likely be great at executing tasks and big projects. It's important to remember, though, that sometimes there isn't time to get every detail right. You'll feel rushed or you'll feel like some people don't understand what it takes to do things right. Have patience.

Researcher and Precision Lover

You love accuracy. You'll never quote a statistic unless you trust that you remember it correctly, trust the source, and trust its timeliness. You're great at working through logical problems and seeing details that might become issues later on.

If this is you, you're great at finding potential solutions to problems. You're great at working with technology, purchasing needed tools, and thinking through processes. It's important to remember, though, that sometimes working with others keeps you from being able to do everything you want to do. Sometimes decisions need to be made faster, even if they're wrong. A bit of humility and remembering that failure isn't final can go a long way in helping you work best with your team.

○ ○ ○

Understand what you bring to the table, and look for opportunities to give your best. You might even consider telling your team leader what you think you can offer. As leaders, we want to know how best to use you on the team. And believe it or not, sometimes we get things wrong. We might assume you have strengths in one area when they're really somewhere completely different. Even physicians get a diagnosis wrong 40 percent of the time, and that's for something physical.[*] When it comes to personality, it's even easier to get it wrong.

[*]Sean Alfano, "Because the Doctor Isn't Always Right," CBS News, May 7, 2006, https://www.cbsnews.com/news/because-the-doctor-isnt-always-right.

Let your leaders know how you best function. Consider taking a personality test and giving them the results. You have permission to be you.

Now, that doesn't mean you won't occasionally be called on to do something that doesn't fit within your unique personality. If you're an encourager, you might be asked to work on some details. If you're a researcher, you might be asked to encourage people by greeting them in the foyer. Serving means laying down your rights, aptitudes, and preferences to accomplish the goal. Even if it's something outside your individuality, you can still bring your unique personality to the task. You can do it in a way nobody else can.

We're all better when we do that. When we bring that special something God has given us to the table, things are better. It's like we're pointing to God and saying, "We see how you've made us. We love it."

Can't you just imagine a team where everyone's working together, bringing their best, and accomplishing a unified goal? That team would be unstoppable. That's the potential you have as a volunteer. You can be part of an unstoppable team.

Try praying for your team this way:

God, I pray I can better understand what I uniquely bring to my team. Help me to be open when asking others how they see me. I want to clearly know how I am wired and what my main contribution is so the team can be remarkable.

4

How Can You Thrive as a Volunteer?

STORY: **Jason**

Oscar was one of my team leaders. He was awesome. He said yes to anything we asked of him, and he gave his all to the task.

While that was part of what made him awesome, that's what also led to the problem. He gave his all, not only to his role in my area of ministry, but also to his roles in other areas of the church. Soon enough, he became exhausted.

Oscar was one of the most reliable volunteers we had, so leaders were naturally attracted to him. They all asked him for stuff. And it's fun to be wanted. It's fun to help out at the church. But before long, the accumulation of yeses caught up with him.

I had to have a talk with him. I suggested he take a breather. Honestly, that was a struggle. He didn't want to let anybody down. But we both knew things couldn't continue how they had been, so he made the change.

After that conversation with him, I could tell his life became lighter. He was able to get some of his breathing space back. And truthfully, what he was giving as a volunteer got better. The things he was able to say yes to got his all.

○ ○ ○

God made us to thrive. Unfortunately, because of our fallen world, thriving isn't our default. Instead, the law of entropy settles into our lives. No matter what we do, unless we approach things with care and intentionality, they start decaying into disorder. Life rarely gets easier. Instead, it gets more complex and more hectic. Then, because we're in an unhealthy place, we give complexity and chaos to others. As Jesus said in Luke 6:45, "Good people do good things because of the good in their hearts. Bad people do bad things because of the evil in their hearts. Your words show what is in your heart" (CEV).

The same is true for volunteering in a church. As great as the church is, as great as your team is, nothing and nobody is perfect. None of us are immune to entropy, to burnout, to not thriving.

Fortunately, there's hope. It's possible to thrive long-term as a volunteer. You never have to go through burnout, disillusionment, or resentment. And if you've found yourself there in the past or are even there now, you can get out. You don't have to be stuck.

Thriving as a volunteer requires some perspective shift. Here are four things to remember as you volunteer.

Serving God is not a replacement for knowing God.

> To love him with all your heart, with all your understanding and with all your strength, and to love your neighbor as yourself is more important than all burnt offerings and sacrifices. (Mark 12:33 NIV)

Families get in trouble all the time because they confuse serving with knowing. For instance, imagine a father who spends all his time working and providing for his children but never spends time with them. Sure, they might dress well and have fun toys, but they won't feel loved. Or imagine a married couple who spends all their time working, maintaining the house, and taking care of the kids, yet they never go on a date night or spend time hearing each other's deepest thoughts. Their relationship is on shaky ground.

We're prone to think that activity for someone takes the place of loving and knowing them. The same can be said for our relationship with God. We want to encourage you: never get so busy serving God that you forget to spend time with him. Read his Word. Spend time in prayer. Let him continue to shape you and give you rest.

Serving is part of your spiritual growth.

> So then, my dear friends, stand firm and steady. Keep busy always in your work for the Lord, since you know that nothing you do in the Lord's service is ever useless. (1 Cor. 15:58 GNT)

As iron sharpens iron,
> so a friend sharpens a friend. (Prov. 27:17 NLT)

Everything we do is spiritual when we do it as unto God, whether it's taking care of kids, scrubbing toilets, parking cars, pushing buttons, or shaking people's hands. The most menial task can have a profound spiritual impact on those we serve and on ourselves. What we invest in others often comes back to us in even greater measure.

Sometimes, though, the process of spiritual formation can feel rough and abrasive. When we serve others but don't feel appreciated . . . when it seems nobody sees what we're doing . . . when people are inadvertently mean to us . . . Those bits of friction can cause us to become either bitter or better. God has put people in our lives to sharpen us and make us more into his image. But we need to see the friction as an opportunity to grow, not as a discouragement.

In serving, you'll become more self-aware. You'll develop your skills. You'll find your limits. These are all opportunities for spiritual growth.

You have gone from being served to serving others.

When a servant comes in from plowing or taking care of sheep, does his master say, "Come in and eat with me"? No, he says, "Prepare my meal, put on your apron, and serve me while I eat. Then you can eat later." (Luke 17:7–8 NLT)

One of the big shifts that needs to happen when you become a volunteer is understanding that church is no longer just about what you get; it's about those you serve. It's like you went from sitting at a table in the restaurant to the kitchen. You're no longer worried about food for yourself. You're cooking food to serve to others. Now, that doesn't mean you don't get to eat. It takes planning and preparation though. You have to serve yourself before or after it's time to serve others.

Prepare yourself to serve others by getting your needs met outside of the time you're serving. Attend a second service (one where you aren't serving). Listen to the recorded message at home so you can get the most from it. Worship in the car on the way to serving. Then be ready to give to others, knowing you've already eaten your fill.

Constantly check your spirit, emotions, and energy.

> Keep your heart with all vigilance,
>> for from it flow the springs of life. (Prov. 4:23)

It's important to analyze yourself every now and then. Give yourself a checkup. Are you tired? Anxious? Tempted? Angry? Be proactive in the way you guard your spirit, emotions, and energy.

It's okay to say no sometimes.

It's okay to ask for help.

It's okay to admit you aren't okay.

When you're a volunteer (or even on staff), it's tempting to pretend everything is perfect. You might be afraid others will judge you as less spiritual or less worthy if you admit you're struggling. But you might be surprised to know how many people in leadership are in counseling, spend evenings crying to their spouse, or need to have hard conversations with accountability partners. No one is perfect, and nobody expects you to be. You can thrive and still be going through some stuff. Be brave enough to reach out for help.

○ ○ ○

We encourage you to evaluate where you are on the thriving spectrum. Maybe you're doing great. You have energy and excitement, and your heart is happy. Guard that. Work to stay that way. Continue to thrive as you serve.

Or maybe you aren't doing great. Maybe it's time to do something to get back to a healthy place. Here are some ideas:

- Get counseling.
- Slow down.
- Read the Bible more.
- Say no to something.
- Talk to a staff person about your struggles.
- Ask for accountability from a fellow volunteer.
- Pray before stepping in to serve.
- Scale back what you've said yes to.

Remember, what's going on in your heart is what you have to give out. So keep that treasure pure. Thrive as a volunteer by having a thriving heart.

We encourage you to pray this prayer:

God, I pray that you would constantly remind me that I need you. I am not perfect. The people on my team are not perfect. Help me to watch my heart. I want to thrive as a volunteer. Help me to focus on you more than on my tasks. May I never become captured by serving so much that I crowd you out.

5

What Is the Best Way
to See Your Team Members?

STORY: **Jonathan**

I volunteered on the tech team at my church, running slides. The sound engineer was on my left, and the lighting designer was on my right. Most often, that lighting designer was Aaron. He was a young guy who had gotten a job in our area, so he'd moved away from family and friends. The church was where he spent most of his time outside of work.

Aaron was good—really good. His lighting designs were absolutely gorgeous. He had a natural eye for it. The only problem was that he wasn't great at taking feedback.

He wasn't rude when pastors or other lighting designers gave him notes. Instead, he would beat himself up over the feedback for the rest of the day. If something went wrong at the beginning of the first service, he'd dwell on it for the next four hours.

I was the one sitting next to him during many of those times. I found out through many conversations with Aaron that he had grown up without strong parental figures in his life. He often had been punished harshly or belittled when he did something wrong. It turned out that his employer treated him much the same way. He was bringing that history and context into his volunteer role at the church.

After the feedback, we were always quick to show Aaron how much we appreciated him. We expressed all of the positive things we saw in him. But he could never hear those. He'd still beat himself up when he made a mistake.

Even though I was just a volunteer with no pastoral authority at church, I found myself counseling Aaron during many services. We unpacked some of the reasons he responded to criticism the way he did. It was a long road to walk, getting him to a place where he could bring his best and still work within the context of feedback from people around him.

○ ○ ○

As much as we love to compartmentalize our lives, things bleed into each other. What we've experienced in the past will often find its way into our future. Past hurts can inform current roles.

The sad truth is that we've all experienced hurts. We've all been unappreciated, taken advantage of, and talked about behind our backs. Maybe you had that in your home growing up.

Or it's currently in your house, in previous volunteer roles, at work, or at school.

If you don't deal with past hurts, they can leave open wounds. Those raw areas can be extra sensitive, even when others don't intend to hurt you. When someone says or does something hurtful, it can be almost impossible to see past what happened previously. *This is the exact same thing that happened before,* you say to yourself. And even if it's completely different, you often see through tainted lenses.

You can't thrive long as a volunteer unless you change your perspective on working with people. Here are three things that can help you see your fellow team members in a healthy way and ensure the longevity of your ability to volunteer.

Look for the good.

> And now, dear brothers and sisters, one final thing. Fix your thoughts on what is true, and honorable, and right, and pure, and lovely, and admirable. Think about things that are excellent and worthy of praise. (Phil. 4:8 NLT)

There's a story told about twin boys. One was an extreme pessimist; the other, an optimist. Their parents decided their birthday was an opportunity to help temper each of their extreme personalities.

The pessimist woke up on his birthday and found his whole room covered in new toys. Everything he possibly could have wanted was in there. Yet he responded, "Oh, they'll probably all break anyway. And do we even have enough batteries for all these toys? This is a disaster." No change.

The optimist woke up and found his room covered in mounds of horse poop. Undaunted, he excitedly started digging through the piles.

His parents exclaimed, "What are you doing? Don't dig in that!"

The child responded, "But with all this poop, there's got to be a pony somewhere!"

Pardon the crass joke, but the principle is sound. Often we see negative things in others, and we take the pessimistic approach. What if, instead, we look for the pony in each one of our team members? Even if we don't understand everything they're doing, we can trust there's something good buried in them. Look for the best in your team leaders and fellow volunteers.

Forgive quickly.

> Be kind and compassionate to one another, forgiving each
> other, just as in Christ God forgave you. (Eph. 4:32 NIV)

We've talked previously about how hurts are inevitable. When you get imperfect people together, friction happens.

Forgive quickly. Life can be unkind, but there's no sense in being unkind to others in the process. Forgive others even when they don't deserve it, just like Jesus modeled for us.

Leave no gaps in communication.

> Know this, my beloved brothers: let every person be quick to hear, slow to speak, slow to anger. (James 1:19)

Communication is imperfect. We can't read one another's minds. So everything we hear and say gets filtered through our past experiences. When people with different experiences are all in one room, misunderstanding happens. There are gaps between what they're trying to say and what we're hearing. Don't let those gaps stay there.

Listen to what people are saying, which sometimes means asking clarifying questions. Be clear about what they are and aren't saying. They may be saying:

- I want you to change how you're doing something.
- I'd like to assign you somewhere else.

They may not be saying:

- I don't value what you've already done.
- You're doing a bad job in your current role.

Don't let simple feedback or casual conversation turn into cause for offense. Confront the issue with love, ask questions, and listen.

○ ○ ○

The simple truth is that everyone has been hurt. And overcoming hurt is not as easy as simply moving on. Sometimes you can't move on. You can only move forward. The hurt will still be there, but you can't allow it to paralyze you. You can't get stuck in it.

Jason's wife is a counselor (we both believe strongly in the power of counseling), and she has the following suggestions to help you if you find yourself seeing your fellow team members through your hurt. Prayerfully work through these:

- Realize everyone has been hurt, including you.
- Be aware of certain triggers. You know the things that set you off.
- Ask, "Where is this hurt coming from?"
- Be encouraged that being hurt doesn't have to keep you stuck.
- Be careful not to let people feel the brunt of the hurt you've experienced.
- Remember that hurt in one area of your life can find its way into other areas.

Here's a prayer to get you started:

God, I pray that my past hurts would not overtake my emotions and friendships. May I be realistic about any hurt, big or small, and move forward. Help me not to get stuck. I want to be free and let those around me experience the best I have and can give.

6

How Can You Be Authentic and Excellent?

STORY: Jonathan

It was the end of the service. "Okay, everyone, let's get back up on stage," I said to the rest of the worship team. "We're going to end this service with a bang."

Our pastor had planned an altar call at the end of the service. He knew it would be high impact, and we couldn't afford to drop the ball. We had to be on our A game.

We heard his cue and made our way on stage. He was delivering an impassioned plea for people to turn their lives toward Jesus. I was just about to put on my guitar when he interrupted his train of thought and said to the congregation, "Come on, guys. I know the band is loud and distracting. But stay with me here."

All eyes were on me, the worship leader, even though the pastor hadn't intended that. He was trying to get people to focus on what he was saying, but everyone was tuning out and staring at the band members taking their places. He didn't mean to humiliate us or sound angry, but I perceived both of those things. It felt horrible.

I could tell the rest of the band felt the exact same way. Yet the click track started and we began to play.

There was no escape. We were on stage. We had a job to do—a very public job. And we still needed to deliver our best.

That was one of the hardest times I've ever had to serve as a volunteer. I felt embarrassed. I felt discouraged. I felt angry. But I still had a job to do. I had to encourage others to worship God even though I didn't feel like it.

○ ○ ○

Hopefully you've never experienced something like that in church. Humiliation is bad enough, but getting embarrassed on stage is mortifying. Trying to give your best when you're feeling like that takes a lot of guts.

Maybe you haven't felt humiliated at church, but we've all walked into church feeling discouraged or tired or distracted. Life does that to all of us. And if we're on the schedule to serve, sometimes those feelings can get in the way of giving our best.

What's the solution? Ignore our feelings and pretend like everything's fine? Operate from our feelings and hope things work out for the best?

Neither of those is a good option. The thing is, feelings do matter. Ignoring them can lead to angry blowups either at church or at home. At the same time, we can't afford to let our feelings become our operating system.

The solution: we speak truth to our feelings.

Truth doesn't say to our feelings, "You don't exist." Truth says, "In spite of what I'm feeling, I will move forward." You decide to do the right thing regardless of what you're feeling.

You might be asking, "Isn't that hypocrisy, though?" If you're anything like us, you're terrified of becoming a hypocritical Christian.

But pretending to be someone you aren't is different from doing the right thing in spite of your feelings. It's never hypocritical to do the right thing. You act in spite of your feelings because you recognize the importance of the responsibility entrusted to you.

God rewards you when you take care of the things he's given you. There are blessings on the other side of your obedience. Here are some of the promises you can expect.

Christ's power will be displayed.

> Each time he said, "My grace is all you need. My power works best in weakness." So now I am glad to boast about my weaknesses, so that the power of Christ can work through me. (2 Cor. 12:9 NLT)

Ever feel like you aren't enough for the task God's given you? Well, maybe you aren't. That's a fortunate thing. First, it shows that you're doing something that's important. Second,

God promises that his power is most evident when you feel weakest.

If you want to be part of a church that's impacting people for eternity, it's going to mean feeling a bit unqualified every now and then. You'll feel inadequate for the role sometimes. But God knows what he wants to accomplish with your church. He has given you all you need to do what he's called you to. You do what you can do, and he'll do what only he can do.

God will use your obedience.

> Father, if you are willing, take this cup from me; yet not my will, but yours be done. (Luke 22:42 NIV)

The above passage comes from the scene where Jesus was praying before he was sent to the cross. He had recently been betrayed. He knew what was coming. It was agonizing for him. He was discouraged. He was tired. Yet we know what happened on the other side of Jesus's obedience: salvation arrived.

Fortunately, you aren't responsible for the salvation of all mankind. You wouldn't be able to survive under the agony of that burden. But perhaps you can see a picture of what's possible when you obey God in spite of how you're feeling.

God can exceed your expectations.

> Now all glory to God, who is able, through his mighty power at work within us, to accomplish infinitely more than we might ask or think. (Eph. 3:20 NLT)

Human beings have tremendous power. We've built cities. We've walked on the moon. We've harnessed atoms. Each of us has amazing potential inside. But guess what? As good as we are, God is greater.

When you choose to do the right thing even when you're distracted, you free yourself of the limitations of your own imagination. You discover even greater things are possible than what you could accomplish alone. God can move, and you get to be a part of that.

○ ○ ○

We can't afford to operate at the level of our feelings. Emotion-driven lives won't bring stability or lead toward a great future. But when we realize that our feelings can change and that we don't have to be a victim to them, God honors our obedience.

Sometimes it just takes speaking the truth to ourselves like David did in the Psalms. David actually spoke to his soul and told it what to do:

> Bless the LORD, O my soul,
> > and all that is within me,
> > bless his holy name!
> Bless the LORD, O my soul,
> > and forget not all his benefits,
> who forgives all your iniquity,
> > who heals all your diseases,
> who redeems your life from the pit,
> > who crowns you with steadfast love and mercy,

who satisfies you with good
so that your youth is renewed like the eagle's. (Ps.
103:1–5)

Next time you walk into church and you just aren't feeling it, we want to encourage you to reset yourself. Acknowledge what you're feeling, then confess the truth. Maybe read Psalm 103 and remember God's goodness. Then choose to obey. Say this simple prayer:

God, I pray you would give me courage to obey you. I may be feeling discouraged and distracted, but I know you have a great plan. I am trusting you to be strong even though I feel weak. After all, you have been preparing me for who you want me to be and what you trust me to do.

7

How Can You Encourage Your Fellow Volunteers?

STORY: **Jason**

My teenage daughter has been going through some tough situations recently. As a father, I was doing my best to help her walk through them. To be honest, though, sometimes it felt like my words were falling on deaf ears. I hoped I was helping her, but you can never be sure.

A few Sundays ago, we were standing and singing at church. The worship team was playing a song that talked about the battle belonging to the Lord. I put my arm around my daughter, leaned over, and whispered, "I know the situation you're in right now. These lyrics are for you."

Tears fell down her cheeks as she leaned into me for the next few songs.

In that moment I was reminded that my words do matter. Even when it feels like I can't make an impact, there is power in my words to provide hope and support. I just had to continue in courage and share them.

o o o

A father's words matter so much to his daughter. Psychology has shown us that fact. But it's easy to believe that our words don't mean anything on the peer level. It's easy to believe that our fellow volunteers won't hear the encouragement we want to give—that our encouragement will fall on deaf ears. That's a lie.

Our words carry power. Proverbs 18:21 tells us, "Death and life are in the power of the tongue." With our words, we can either infuse life into someone or contribute to death and decay in their world. It's so important to acknowledge that responsibility.

Because of that, you have an opportunity for leadership on your volunteer team. Again, whether you have the title or not, you can lead others. Why not lead them toward encouragement?

We want to encourage you to look for signs that indicate your fellow volunteers need encouragement. You might find them in one of the following situations, so look for opportunities to speak life into their world.

A Fellow Volunteer Who Seems Lazy

Set an example for the believers in speech, in conduct, in love, in faith and in purity. (1 Tim. 4:12 NIV)

Unfortunately, if a fellow volunteer seems lazy or like they aren't pulling their weight, there isn't really a great way to approach the situation directly. Calling someone out will most often lead to hurt or defensiveness. There is, however, a way to encourage them indirectly. In Matthew 10:16, Jesus told us to "be wise as serpents and innocent as doves." Our goal isn't to manipulate someone but to understand the best way to motivate them.

Try the following steps:

1. *Model excellence.* Don't let their laziness provoke you to laziness. Instead, continue working hard. People notice that.

2. *Encourage what you see in them.* Point out the great things they do or the potential you see in them. Again, don't manipulate. Encourage. You might even acknowledge something you see in their personality type that you find valuable.

3. *Invite them along.* If you're tackling a problem or doing something above and beyond the call of duty, invite them to join you. Everyone loves to feel needed and important. By including them instead of discounting them, you give them a reputation to live up to.

Often, people get lazy because nobody notices or they don't feel the importance of a task. So when *you* notice, it gives them incentive to work harder.

A Fellow Volunteer Who Feels Discouraged

> Everyone enjoys a fitting reply;
>> it is wonderful to say the right thing at the right
>> time! (Prov. 15:23 NLT)

It's much easier to encourage a peer who feels discouraged, but you still have to do it the right way. Encouragement without truly understanding can come across as dismissive. Instead, try the following steps:

1. *Listen and hear them out.* Repeat back what you hear to ensure you're actually understanding what they feel.
2. *Remind them.* Encourage them with why you're volunteering—who you're serving. Maybe think back to a success story they had as a volunteer and remind them of that.
3. *Be on their side.* Reassure them that you're on their team. You're in this together and they are not alone.

You can't shift someone from discouraged to encouraged in just one day. It will take time. But small steps in the right direction can lead to huge results.

A Fellow Volunteer Who Feels Hurt

If your brother sins against you, go and tell him his fault, between you and him alone. If he listens to you, you have gained your brother. But if he does not listen, take one or two others along with you, that every charge may be established by the evidence of two or three witnesses. (Matt. 18:15–16)

The unfortunate truth about working with people is that hurts happen. As we said earlier, people hurt people (most often, unintentionally). So there's a good chance one of your fellow volunteers will deal with hurt at some point in their journey.

The above Scripture is talking about sin, but the model works well for any hurt. It's too easy to talk about the other person or let an offense grow into bitterness. You have the opportunity to help your fellow volunteer deal with their hurt and process it in an appropriate way.

Here are some steps to help:

1. *Acknowledge their pain, but don't assume.* You can say, "That must feel horrible," but never assume you have all the facts. Don't fall into the trap of taking an offense that isn't yours to bear.

2. *Encourage them to confront the issue.* Ask, "Have you talked to the person about it?" You don't have to be heavy-handed, reminding them of what Jesus said in Matthew 18. But you can gently lead them to the right steps.

3. *Encourage them in forgiveness.* Say, "Don't let this feeling ruin your day. Unforgiveness won't help the situation, and it will hurt you if you hold on to it." Offer to pray

with them or suggest they talk to a professional who can help in the situation.

○ ○ ○

It's unfortunate that people get hurt in church. The beautiful thing, though, is that we can help one another and lead one another to forgiveness. The fruit of the Spirit is best worked out in conflict and in our fellow brothers and sisters in Christ encouraging us toward love and good works.

You have the opportunity to be part of that for your fellow team members. You can inspire them, encourage them, and lead them to forgiving those who hurt them.

In preparation for your next time volunteering, we encourage you to pray this prayer:

Lord, give me an opportunity to extend your encouragement to my fellow volunteers. I want to help them last for the long haul. As you teach me to navigate the complications of relationships and serving, I pray you would help me care for others so they can do the same.

8

Does What You Do Matter?

The Bible is filled with encouragement. It's one of the best books to dive into when you need to get a proper perspective on life. But there are times when the Bible can get a bit depressing. Look at Ecclesiastes, for instance. King Solomon was going through some pretty intense feelings when he wrote that book. It opens like this: "In my opinion, nothing is worthwhile; everything is futile. For what does a man get for all his hard work? Generations come and go, but it makes no difference" (1:2–4 TLB).

Have you ever felt like everything is meaningless? That nothing matters? That there's nothing new in this world?

If we're being honest, we could probably all admit to feeling like that at some point in our lives. Perhaps you've felt:

- Nobody notices what I do.
- I don't feel seen.
- What I'm doing doesn't even matter.

- I'm not needed.
- What am I even doing?

Maybe you've felt that way with your job. You wonder if your work has any meaning to it. *Would anyone even notice if I switched jobs? Does my work make a lasting impact on anyone?*

Or maybe you've felt that way in your relationships. You wonder if you'll ever stop fighting with your spouse or if unhealthy patterns will ever change. *Will we ever get to a good place?*

Or maybe you've felt that in volunteering. *Is what I'm doing important? Am I making an impact at church? Would my team miss me if I wasn't there?*

Those are perfectly normal feelings. We all want to feel like we're needed and our input matters. Nobody wants to feel like the hamster spinning on its wheel—lots of activity but ultimately no forward progress.

Parenting is one of those jobs that feels futile. It's a lot of grinding in the beginning. Cleaning diapers, barely sleeping, feeding fussy babies . . . Then those babies turn into toddlers, and it can seem like you're just yelling at them all day. It's easy to feel like you're doing a horrible job and that you'll never get out of this phase.

At the same time, nobody would say that a parent's job is futile. We all know the importance of parenting. We know it's an investment. And we all know that things eventually change. Children outgrow different phases. But when you're in the middle of the battle, it's hard to see that.

That's the way it is with so many areas of our lives. Because of our season in life, we feel like things don't matter, but we would never say that about someone else who was in the same situation. It's easy to see perspective for others but hard to see for ourselves.

When we feel this way, it's easy to get stuck, to stop forward progress in our lives. But we can't afford to stay where we are. We have to move forward in spite of not feeling it. We don't devalue what we feel, but we do move forward.

We want to remind you that what you do does matter. As a volunteer, no matter how public or invisible your role might be, you are making a difference. You are a part of something important.

What you do matters for the atmosphere of your church.

Even so the body is not made up of one part but of many.

Now if the foot should say, "Because I am not a hand, I do not belong to the body," it would not for that reason stop being part of the body. And if the ear should say, "Because I am not an eye, I do not belong to the body," it would not for that reason stop being part of the body. If the whole body were an eye, where would the sense of hearing be? If the whole body were an ear, where would the sense of smell be? But in fact God has placed the parts in the body, every one of them, just as he wanted them to be. If they were all one part, where would the body be? As it is, there are many parts, but one body. (1 Cor. 12:14–20 NIV)

In the above passage, Paul talks about the church as a body. He compares it with the human body as a way to illustrate the importance of each and every one of us.

A beautiful thing about our bodies is that there's a lot of redundancy. There are two eyes, two ears, two feet, multiple fingers . . . There are only a few parts that, if lost, would cause our bodies to cease functioning. We could lose an ear or an eye or a foot and still function. But each of those parts adds an important element to life. We can get by with one eye, but things look flat. We can get by with one ear, but it's harder to separate sounds. Each body part changes the atmosphere for us.

The same is true for your church. Bodies change the atmosphere. Even if they're just sitting in a seat, bodies make a difference.

Think about a comedy club. If you walked in and nobody was there, what would your expectations be for that show? You probably wouldn't expect much. You wouldn't expect it to be good. But a packed room sets an atmosphere of expectation, especially if people are engaged in the moment. Their presence matters.

The same is true for you. If nothing else, just your very presence matters for the room.

What you do matters for your team.

Here's another way to put it: You're here to be light, bringing out the God-colors in the world. (Matt. 5:14 Message)

STORY: **Jason**

A while back, I was approached by one of my volunteers. She had tears in her eyes as she told me, "You don't know this, but I've been going through a divorce. Nobody on the team knows it either. But the thing that's been holding me together through this whole time has been this team. I'm going to tell them today."

Her words illustrated how important we are to our fellow team members. Some people are hanging on by a thread, but our presence is enough to keep them connected.

I knew there were people coming in, volunteering, feeling like what they were doing didn't matter. But for this one soul, what they did made all the difference.

You have no idea what impact your presence is making on your fellow team members. Your prayer, your smile, your attitude—they might be the thing helping someone get through a hard day.

What you do matters for you.

> Give, and it will be given to you. A good measure, pressed down, shaken together and running over, will be poured into your lap. For with the measure you use, it will be measured to you. (Luke 6:38 NIV)

There's something that happens inside us when we do something for someone who can't do anything for us in return. Helping others can break through discouragement. There's joy in

57

giving. It also helps reset our perspective from an internal one to an external one.

But the biggest truth is that there's a principle God set up in his economy. When we give, our generosity comes back to us, even if it's in a different way. We might encourage someone, and then we find encouragement coming to us from a completely different source. Or we might invest finances somewhere, then see those finances return to us from somewhere else. It's a principle God created.

So when you need encouragement or joy or love or friendship, your responsibility is to invest it in someone else. When you do that, without demanding anything in return, you get it back.

Your volunteering matters to you, because it's an investment that will return to you.

What you do matters to God.

> Therefore, my beloved brothers, be steadfast, immovable, always abounding in the work of the Lord, knowing that in the Lord your labor is not in vain. (1 Cor. 15:58)

Nothing you do for God is ever done in vain, because God sees everything. Whether or not you ever get appreciation or credit here on earth, you can trust that God is keeping track. He will reward you.

God has entrusted us with a divine responsibility. We are to be atmosphere setters. Matthew 5:14 tells us that our job is to be light, which brings out colors. The previous verse calls us salt, which brings out flavors. We were meant to impact the world by changing its core essence.

You have that responsibility and that power; God has already given them to you.

○ ○ ○

Your light has a ripple effect to people all around. You're setting an atmosphere for your pastors, for your fellow volunteers, for your church, and even for yourself. Never forget that opportunity. Never forget that what you do matters.

We encourage you to ask God to remind you of the importance of what you're doing as a volunteer. Use this short prayer as a starter:

God, I pray you would show me the impact of what I'm doing. Even when I feel like nobody sees what I do, I know you see. Bring to my mind the people you've given me the opportunity to impact. Don't let me lose sight of the individuals you love. Reinforce my burden to love those you love.

9

What Should Relationships with Fellow Volunteers Look Like?

STORY: **Jonathan**

Hi, I'm Jonathan. I embrace shallow relationships.

I'm not necessarily a shallow person. I do believe in deep relationships. At the same time, though, I tend to make friends with everyone. As long as you don't lie to me or make me miserable when we hang out, I generally like you. I have hundreds of friends, but that tends to lend itself to shallow relationships. There's not much time to talk about more than weather or sports when you're friends with everyone. My friends and I tend to laugh and have a good time, then I forget about them until the next time I see them.

I know you're judging me, and I'm okay with that.

I've had to learn that not every relationship should be a shallow relationship. I need to have depth. Whenever I go through tough times in my life, they test my need for depth. As long as everything's going great, shallow friendships are fine. But when I'm going through a dark time, that's when I need someone who will be there for me no matter what. That's when I need deeper relationships.

At the same time, I'm also learning that not everyone needs to be considered a friend. There are relationships in my life that are cordial and transactional, but they don't go beyond that. That's okay too.

○ ○ ○

Chances are you fall somewhere on this spectrum:

- Everyone is your friend.
- Few people make it past your friendship gate.

You probably aren't as extreme as either of those, but you likely lean more toward one or the other.

Relationships are important. In fact, most of what Jesus said to the disciples had to do with their relationships to one another. He spent a lot of time telling his team to humble themselves and treat one another more kindly. Writers like Paul and John echoed those thoughts in their letters in the New Testament.

If we're going to do church right, we have to do relationships right, because that's the model set forth for us in the Bible. The problem is, healthy relationships are nuanced. The two approaches above don't lead to success. There has to be a balanced approach.

We've seen four levels of relationships in volunteer teams. These levels require different things from you, but they'll also give you certain things that other levels of relationships won't.

Checked Out

There are some who walk in and out of church without ever affecting others or being affected by them. Obviously, this doesn't describe you. You are already plugged in, volunteering.

But if we aren't careful, we can all have seasons of this in our lives. Maybe we roll into church, perform our task, do the bare minimum, and go back home as if nothing happened. This doesn't lead to healthy relationships.

Transactional

My brothers and sisters, believers in our glorious Lord Jesus Christ must not show favoritism. Suppose a man comes into your meeting wearing a gold ring and fine clothes, and a poor man in filthy old clothes also comes in. If you show special attention to the man wearing fine clothes and say, "Here's a good seat for you," but say to the poor man, "You stand there" or "Sit on the floor by my feet," have you not discriminated among yourselves and become judges with evil thoughts? (James 2:1–4 NIV)

The next level is transactional. The majority of people in your life fall into this category. You know them. You're nice to them. You treat them fairly. You give to them minimally, and they give minimally in return. If they seem discouraged, you might smile at them or give them an encouraging word. If they do something good, you'll celebrate with them. You might talk to them midweek to get things done or when you have specific questions, but that's about it. This is the shallow level of relationships, and there's nothing wrong with it.

In this level of relationship, it's important not to treat some better than others. You don't show preference to those who can benefit you in the future, and you don't burn bridges just because you think a relationship won't serve you later.

At the same time, you won't reveal secrets about yourself. You won't go to these people for deep life advice.

It's good to have these types of relationships in your life, but they can't end there.

Friendship

> Oil and perfume make the heart glad,
>> and the sweetness of a friend comes from his
>> earnest counsel. (Prov. 27:9)

> Walk with the wise and become wise,
>> for a companion of fools suffers harm. (Prov.
>> 13:20 NIV)

The next level of relationship on your volunteer team is friendship. These are the people you want to hang out with during the week. They're the ones to whom you'll tell deeper truths about yourself. They'll know you pretty well. And they'll be there for you when you're going through tough times. They'll be the ones to bring you casseroles when you have a death in the family or welcome a new baby into the world. You'll hang out during the week and talk about things outside of Sunday.

This level of relationship requires a certain amount of trust, so not everyone needs to be here. But you can have quite a few friends. It's not *that* exclusive of a group.

In this level, it's important you don't exclude people who aren't a part of your friendship group. You can still include people in activities even though they aren't part of your inner circle. A healthy team is inclusive, even though people will cluster into groups of similar personalities and interests.

This is where most people end on the spectrum. They have friends but nothing deeper. Fortunately, there's one more level.

Life Exchange

> A friend loves at all times,
>> and a brother is born for adversity. (Prov. 17:17)

Life-exchange friendships are rare. They're almost completely (ideally, completely) transparent. There are no secrets, and no area of your life is off-limits. A friend at this level can tell you the hard truths and you'll accept them, because you know that their heart is for you.

You'll probably only have one to three people at this level of relationship. Few people on your team can be this type of friend for you, but it's important to find someone who can. It's also important, though, to use wisdom in this. Life-exchange friendships are highly connective. There needs to be trust but also prudence. For instance, a married man might not get to this level of friendship with a single woman. It could be unwise or inappropriate to do so.

But the right kind of intimacy is great. We shouldn't be afraid to get intimate in our relationships, because we all become better when we have this level of friendship in our lives.

○ ○ ○

Regardless of where your relationships fall, it's important to realize that you have an amount of pastoral influence at each level. You can impact others. At the shallow level, you can offer encouragement and wise advice. At the friendship level, you can watch out for things that might trip up your friends or see if they're walking away from the truth of God. At the deepest level, you're directly helping them become the person God has created them to be.

Your team leader will do things to help foster different levels of relationships on your team, but it's important to realize that relationship is your responsibility. What you put into friendship is what you'll get out of it. You can't wait for staff or team leaders to do all the work of relationships.

That means if someone is in the hospital, you have the opportunity to visit them. If someone needs a meal delivered, you get to do that. You can even organize the event.

Relationships aren't hierarchical. They're organic and crisscross and messy, and that's what makes them beautiful. That's the beauty of the church: we're all different races, ages, backgrounds, and abilities, coming together in relationship to walk this faith journey.

We encourage you to think through the relationships on your team. What have you been getting from your relationships, and what have you been giving? Think through the members of your team and evaluate which level each person is at. Are they in the right place? Do you need to promote someone to the level of life exchange?

Relationships are the key to longevity in life, so make sure you are incorporating them into your life. Establish relationships that lead you where God has you going. Ask him to help:

God, I pray I would be a kind friend to people around me. There is no way to know what people are going through, and I could be a helpful voice or a listening ear for them. Help me to be open and sensitive to the type of friendship that others want and I need.

10

How Can You Understand Priorities and Seasons in Your Life?

STORY: **Jason**

I've found myself in a new role recently. I accepted a new job. That's changed some dynamics with my family, church, and career.

I've been asked to go on a trip this week. Normally, that wouldn't be a problem, but my daughter has an event on Friday evening. It'll be her last time cheerleading with her team. They're doing a new routine, and I know it's important to her that I be there. Now I'm having to figure out how to balance this trip with being there for my daughter. Regardless of how well I do, I know something is going to lose this week. New pressures in my life will cause me to fail at least one group. Which one will it be?

○ ○ ○

You've probably found yourself in this sort of conflict. Maybe you started a new job, and that's changing the dynamics with your family. Or maybe volunteering is changing some things with a weekend work schedule.

We're all trying to figure out how to survive the immediate. We're trying to cope with the "right now." But when juggling multiple priorities, there always comes a point when we have to choose one priority over another. What happens when all your priorities collide? How do you choose?

We have limited resources—money, time, energy—and for one thing to win, something else has to lose. This can lead to feelings of guilt, because sometimes important things have to lose. Sometimes good things conflict with each other.

Fortunately, there's a bit of hope when you change your perspective on things. Our friend Pastor Daniel Villarreal says it like this: "Something will always lose in your life. That's okay. As long as it's not the same thing that loses every time."

Your spouse shouldn't always lose. Your children shouldn't always lose. Your career, your church, volunteering—if these priorities are losing every time, something needs to change. When you're able to balance priorities, you can make sure that things are getting your attention at the right time.

Often, people have priority structures in their lives that are absolute. Many people's priority structures look like this:

1. God
2. Spouse
3. Family

4. Career

5. Church

6. Entertainment

Note: "God" and "church" can be confusing because we often experience God inside church services. But things beyond the critical elements like God's teaching, fellowship, breaking bread, and prayer get a lower priority—things like serving and attending extra events.

This is a pretty healthy structure. But some people approach their priority list in an all-or-nothing fashion. Their spouse gets 100 percent of their attention, so anything that conflicts with their spouse gets a "no." Or worse, if priorities are misplaced, the career will get 100 percent and everything else will suffer.

A balanced approach to priorities acknowledges that even sometimes those things that are higher up won't get the attention they deserve. Nothing should consistently lose. For instance, you wouldn't constantly choose your spouse at the expense of your children. You wouldn't sacrifice church consistently to benefit your career.

However, there are seasons when building a career requires your family getting a little bit less of you than you'd like. For a month or two, that's fine. The problem is when it becomes a long-term situation. Sacrificing your family for ten years while you build your career might ensure they aren't there when those ten years are up.

Rhythms are an important concept in life. It's vital to understand how things change from season to season.

The first thing to remember is that you can serve God without serving the church. And you can serve the church without serving God. You don't need to serve in a church to serve God, but that's a great way to do it. At the same time, your heart has to be positioned toward serving God, not just completing yet another obligation. Keeping this straight can help you balance your energy when it comes to volunteering.

Second of all, make sure you are serving your family even while you're serving God. God has outlined the role of fathers and mothers, parents and children, and it's important that we fulfill our duties in those realms. If obedience to the things God has already told us to do is more important than sacrifice in serving him (see 1 Sam. 15:22), then we need to take care of our families. Just as we've seen people prioritize family over serving at church, we've also seen people prioritize serving at church over family. Sometimes it's harder to serve your family because it's expected, and you don't get celebrated when you do what is merely expected of you. But make sure your family doesn't get what's left over at the end of serving at church.

At the same time, serving together can be one of the greatest things for your family. Prioritizing church attendance and serving God through the local church can help establish priorities for your kids and also give you and your spouse a shared purpose that's greater than just your family unit.

We want to encourage you to evaluate the different priorities in your life. Has one area been suffering consistently? Have you been neglecting something important at the top of the list or something that, while lower on the list, is still very important?

Here are some practical ideas to help you bring back some balance to your priorities if you find yourself neglecting one area consistently.

God

- Prioritize prayer. Martin Luther once said, "I have so much to do that I shall spend the first three hours in prayer."* Martin Luther allowed God to show him what was most important to help him order his day.
- Prioritize reading Scripture. Relationship involves knowing someone's heart, and God has revealed his heart in his Word.
- Prioritize solitude and godly community. We need both of these in our lives. One helps us hear from God; the other allows God to sharpen us through other people.

Spouse or Significant Other

- Find a way your spouse or significant other can serve with you. This kills two birds with one stone and can help bond you together even more.
- Prioritize date night. When you've filled your spouse's love tank (see Gary Chapman's *The Five Love*

---

*Martin Luther, quoted in James Gilchrist Lawson, *Cyclopedia of Religious Anecdotes* (Grand Rapids: Revell, 1923), 303.

Languages), it's much easier for your spouse to be excited when you serve at church.

- Tell your significant other about your desire to serve God, and ask their opinion. Bring them into your decisions instead of just telling them what you're thinking.

Kids

- Prioritize serving, and have your kids join in.
- Change the conversation at home when communicating about church. Make sure your words reflect that it's an opportunity, not an obligation.
- Introduce them to the people you serve with.
- Have them help out alongside you if possible.

Career

- Consider rejecting the promotion that might contribute to a long-term imbalance in your priorities.
- Reach out to people in your church who navigate career and volunteering to see how they do it.

Church

- It might be time to take a step back from serving for a season. The door will always be open for you if you leave gracefully.

- Maybe it's time to step up and serve more for one season.

○ ○ ○

Ask God to make one of the above ideas stand out to you as you read through them again. Proverbs 16:9 says, "We can make our plans, but the LORD determines our steps" (NLT). You could spend forever trying to arrange your priorities and never get them right. But when you ask God to direct your steps, you can trust he knows what needs your attention when. Don't just follow your own plan. Fall in love with the one who knows the plans and wants to guide you. "Seek first the kingdom of God and his righteousness, and all these things will be added to you" (Matt. 6:33).

The truth is, we all function best when our priorities are in the right place and are getting the right attention. For instance, when a team member's marriage is successful, they'll give better at church. They'll have more energy, more focus, and more time to devote to serving. We all get better when we're all healthy.

We encourage you to pray this prayer:

God, I pray I would be reminded that you know what is going on in my life. Nothing catches you by surprise, even though I often feel like that. I am not always sure of my decisions. Help me to recognize the season I am in and connect with people who can walk alongside me and be a voice in my life. Help me to look to you as I learn to follow you each day.

11

What Can You Do When You Have an Idea for the Team?

STORY: **Jonathan**

I was working at a growing church. A year earlier, we had made the move from one to two services so we could make room for people. Now we were in the same position. We had to make more room by adding an additional service.

I'd done the research. I knew the preferred service times for churches that had three services—9:00 a.m., 10:30 a.m., and noon. So in our staff meeting, I spoke up. "I think we should make these our new service times."

The rest of the team wasn't on board. Nobody on the team thought folks would come to a church service at noon. And truthfully, I don't think any of our staff wanted to get out of service that late. They'd be starving, working through lunch. So we opted for something like 8:00, 9:30, and 11:00.

I knew this was a bad idea. Nobody would come to the 8:00 service. And I was right.

I kept pushing the team to change the service times. Instead, they brought out ideas like offering breakfast or asking people to commit to the earlier time.

Nothing worked, so we made the shift to thirty minutes later. That helped a bit, but that first service was still so empty.

Finally, about a year later, we adopted the service times I'd originally proposed.

I'd like to say I was mature about it, but I wasn't. I said to everyone on the staff, "I told you so." That didn't win me any good-will with my fellow team members, but I felt great for being right.

○ ○ ○

We've all been in situations like this. Maybe you had an idea for your work, your family, or your church. Maybe you had an outside perspective nobody else had (it's easy for people to get too close to a problem). Or maybe you had some unique knowledge or skill that showed you a solution nobody else could see. So you suggested your idea.

If your story is like the one above, your idea may have met resistance. Nobody seemed to embrace or listen to it. So others ignored your best pleas and went with what they thought best.

This can be frustrating, and it can lead to one of two extreme responses. Either you become hesitant to share your ideas in the future, or you become a bulldozer who fights for every opinion.

The world does need your ideas. If you've felt hesitant to share them in the past, we want to encourage you to start now.

If you've become a bulldozer with your opinions, we want to encourage you to approach sharing them in a different way. It's possible to present your ideas more gently *and* get people to listen to them.

The key, though, is that your idea has to be positioned as the best thing for the team and not just a reflection of your preferences. So many suggestions in ministry have to do with preference. Some people prefer different styles of music, or different types of ministry they've seen at other churches, or different paint colors, or different designs . . . There are thousands of differences in preference, and none of them are right or wrong. But we can't allow our preferences to lead our suggestions; otherwise we'll feel like nobody ever listens to us.

However, if you have an idea for a solution to a problem your team faces, it's important to share that. If you notice a pattern that needs to change, address it.

That said, people are generally resistant to change. If you want to share your ideas with your team leader or other members of the team, there's a smart way to go about it. Look at the following steps as guidelines for how to give your ideas their best chance at survival.

1. Support your team leader first.

Obey your leaders and submit to them, for they are keeping watch over your souls, as those who will have to give an account. Let them do this with joy and not with groaning, for that would be of no advantage to you. (Heb. 13:17)

Scripture talks about honoring those who lead us. The verse above even says that your presence should be a joy for them, not something that makes them groan with dread. Start by becoming a joy to your team leader. Become great at listening to them. Excel in the tasks they give you. In a leader's mind, this earns you the right to speak your opinion. When they see how much you're focused on helping them excel, they'll see that your suggestion might benefit them.

You've heard the quote: people won't care how much you know until they know how much you care. When your leader knows how much you care, they'll care about what you know.

Start here. This will give you clout to leverage your idea.

2. Collaborate with your leader.

> Two people are better off than one, for they can help each other succeed. (Eccles. 4:9 NLT)

When you approach your leader, focus on a problem, not a person. Identify systems or situations that are causing obstacles. Problems are projects; people are battles. We don't want to start battles on our teams.

Next, approach the situation from a team perspective. It's not a problem *you* have or *your leader* has; it's a problem *we* have. Now, we aren't recommending manipulative verbiage. Make sure you're actually addressing a problem that affects everyone. Then come alongside your leader to help them solve it.

Finally, provide a potential solution. Remember that your idea isn't the only option, but it's one. Ask if they'd be willing to try an experiment. Start with a small suggestion that won't create a ton of extra work for your team leader. Ideally, you can offer to spearhead the idea and do the work to make it happen.

3. Collaborate with your team.

> Where there is no guidance, a people falls,
>   but in an abundance of counselors there is safety.
>   (Prov. 11:14)

If your leader is open to your idea, that doesn't suddenly give you blanket authority. You still have to continually submit your idea to your leader, and you also have to be a part of helping sell the idea to your team. Remember, you're in the trenches with them, so bring them along in the idea with you.

Part of bringing other people along on the journey is opening up your idea to feedback. Since it's about making the team better, the idea needs to flex to meet the team's unique needs. You also have to be willing not to get the credit if the idea succeeds.

Let the idea win, not you, so that the team can win.

4. Move forward.

> No, dear brothers and sisters, I have not achieved it, but I focus on this one thing: Forgetting the past and looking forward to what lies ahead. (Phil. 3:13 NLT)

Finally, if at any step along this journey you get told no, or if the idea doesn't work out like you hoped it would, you have to be willing to move forward. If your idea is rejected, don't keep pushing for it. Also, don't say "I told you so" if you were right about the need for a solution. It might make you feel better in the short term, but it won't encourage people to listen to your ideas in the future. Let the idea sit, remove your ego from it, and it might resurface later.

There is so much more ahead of us than behind, and we have to be willing to hold all our ideas loosely. We are ultimately advancing God's kingdom and agenda, not our own. We have to remember that we are one small part of one small church that's part of the worldwide movement of the body of Christ.

○ ○ ○

We want to encourage you to give your very best on your team. Give your ideas. Jump in with a sense of ownership. But ultimately trust that God has the big picture in mind, and he will accomplish his purposes.

Use this prayer to align yourself with God's big picture:

God, give me wisdom to pray through the ideas I have and not just shout them out to others. Help me to be all in while slowly leading and influencing others to consider options. If my ideas are not embraced, help me to assume a posture of humility and avoid a negative attitude.

12

How Can You Grow into Leadership?

There's a good chance that if you picked up this book and read this far, you want to move into a place of leadership at some point in your church. Perhaps you want to be on staff, be a volunteer leader, or simply have more influence on your team. Know this: there's nothing wrong with wanting to lead. It's actually a good thing. There are great reasons for it. Aside from God directly telling you, "I want you to be a leader," some of the reasons include:

- You have skills that are underutilized on your team, and you'd like to use them.
- You see something on the team or in the church that could be done better, and you think you know how to do it.
- There isn't a leader currently in a certain position, and you think there needs to be. You happen to have the skills for that position.

- Peers are nudging you, suggesting you should have a leadership role.

The problem is that sometimes things can be awkward when it comes to this desire to lead. Maybe there's someone currently in that leadership position, and it looks like they won't be going anywhere anytime soon. Maybe you feel like nobody notices that you have the leadership skills needed. Or maybe it just would be awkward to tell someone in authority that you want to lead.

For whatever reason, you may feel blocked from your desire to lead. In those moments, it can be tempting to try to take the position by force, manipulate people to get it, or simply grumble and complain that things aren't happening for you.

We know someone who found himself in this exact situation.

David felt a desire to lead on his team, and there was really only one role that seemed right for him—the team leader. For a long time, people had seen his leadership skills and were encouraging him to do something with them.

David became one of the most faithful members of his team. He supported the leader with every ounce of his energy and creativity. The problem was, the team leader didn't like David. In fact, he resented him. He knew what other people were saying, and he didn't want David to have a chance to take his position.

A long time went by, and David found himself stuck. He didn't seem any closer to leadership than when he'd first started out. The crazy thing was that his leader made many public mistakes. David had numerous opportunities to criticize his leader and easily take over his position, but he refused. He believed that if God had called him to lead, God would make it happen at the right time.

Of course, we're talking about the David of the Bible. His leader was King Saul, who even tried to kill David multiple times. Regardless, David refused to raise a hand against his king. We know the end result of that: God promoted David.

Now, you probably aren't trying to be a king at your church or in your job, but the principle of authority in David's story holds true no matter how big or small the position is.

David had the skills, but he waited.

People knew David had the skills, but he waited.

People wanted him to be in charge, but he waited.

Saul refused to leave his leadership position, but David waited.

The timeline probably didn't match what David thought it should look like, but he still waited.

In the right time, God put him in the right position.

There are a few things to learn from David about how to position yourself for promotion into leadership. You can start right now, even if a leadership position seems impossible. Here's how.

1. Own the amount of influence you *do* have.

> One who is faithful in a very little is also faithful in much, and one who is dishonest in a very little is also dishonest in much. (Luke 16:10)

Lead in the capacity you do have. For the people who already look to you as a leader, honor that responsibility. Be the best leader you can be, and help make their lives easier. God loves to see how we manage small responsibilities, because he knows that's how we'll manage large ones.

David began by managing his father's sheep. Then he managed soldiers he was put in charge of. His influence grew as he took each responsibility seriously.

2. Support the current leader.

> So whatever you wish that others would do to you, do also to them, for this is the Law and the Prophets. (Matt. 7:12)

Serve your team leader the way you would want your team to serve you if you were their leader. If you find a way to make your leader's job easier, do it! Just like we talked about in the last chapter, people care about what you want when they know how much you care about what they want. Perhaps your leadership position won't be taking over for your current leader; maybe it will be coming alongside them and serving in a brand-new capacity created just for you. Your faithfulness will open doors for that.

3. Honor your leader publicly and privately.

> The elders who direct the affairs of the church well are worthy of double honor, especially those whose work is preaching and teaching. (1 Tim. 5:17 NIV)

The above verse talks about how good leaders deserve double the amount of honor. But guess what? That implies that even bad leaders are worthy of your honor. Your mama said it this way: if you can't say anything nice, don't say anything at all.

It can be tempting to criticize leadership. But future leaders don't have that luxury. We're meant to honor those above us, even if we don't always feel like it. Again, our goal is to be the type of team member that we'd want to lead one day. Honor goes a long way.

4. Trust that your team sees, leadership sees, and ultimately God sees.

> I know all the things you do. I have seen your love, your faith, your service, and your patient endurance. And I can see your constant improvement in all these things. (Rev. 2:19 NLT)

Trust that the right people are seeing the way you're responding to a situation. Your team sees. And every right decision you make builds more rapport with those you might lead one day.

Also, leadership sees. Your direct leader definitely notices, but even those above them do. They might not act immediately on what they see, however. In fact, sometimes great leaders want to see how people operate under pressure before entrusting them with more responsibility.

Finally, trust that God sees. He has a timeline for your life. It might not look like yours, but it's the best timeline there could be.

○ ○ ○

We encourage you to read the story of David and Saul in 1 Samuel 16–31. There's a good chance you aren't dealing with an evil king like Saul. In fact, your leader is probably a great person who loves you. You may need to position your heart toward the leader, not toward what you aren't getting.

Pray and ask God to help:

God, I want a heart of patience and humility. I want to serve others well with the authority I have been given. I want to trust that what you see in secret will be rewarded publicly, and that is better than anything anyone else could do for me. Help me to be patient in the process.

Jason Young is a hospitality and leadership coach and communicator. He was formerly the director of guest experience at Buckhead Church and North Point Ministries, a nationally known network of churches with 36,000 people in average weekly attendance. He has also worked with numerous organizations, including Ford Motor Company, Life.Church, and Chick-fil-A. Jason has written for numerous publications and enjoys creating the Saturday Rundown, a Saturday morning email with practical ideas on hospitality and leadership. Learn more at jasonyounglive.com. He lives in Atlanta, Georgia.

Jonathan Malm runs SundaySocial.tv and ChurchStageDesign Ideas.com, reaching more than 70,000 church leaders each month. He has begun multiple businesses and consults with churches regularly on guest services and creative expression. You can find him in San Antonio, Texas, writing, cooking, and drinking way too much coffee. Jonathan's first church leadership book, *Unwelcome*, is available on Amazon in print and digital forms. He and Jason are also the authors of *The Come Back Effect* and *The Volunteer Effect*.

JASON YOUNG

Hospitality and Leadership Communicator

JasonYoungLive.com

**COACHING, TRAINING TOOLS, AND ACTIONABLE
RESOURCES FOR THE MODERN-DAY LEADER.**

- Personal or Team
  Coaching
- Keynote Talks
- Half- and Full-Day
  Workshops

- Podcast
- Digital Resource
  Library
- Weekly Hospitality and
  Leadership Rundown

 JY@JasonYoungLive.com

⑤ SUNDAYSOCIAL.TV

SundaySocial.tv (a resource from Jonathan Malm) creates at least two new graphics each day for your church to use on social media. There's a verse-of-the-day graphic that mirrors the Bible App's verse and tons of content to help your church get more likes, comments, shares, and retweets. Get instant access for a low monthly cost.

CHURCH <u>STAGE DESIGN</u> IDEAS

Looking to update your church stage? Check out this free resource from Jonathan Malm, where hundreds of churches from around the world share pictures of and do-it-yourself information about their own church stages. Visit **churchstagedesignideas.com**.

"Pining Away" by Andrew Hunt

"Glowing Hives" by Echo Church

TURN A TEMPORARY VISITOR INTO AN
ENGAGED CHURCH MEMBER

Written by a church consultant and a hospitality expert, *The Come Back Effect* shows you the secret to helping a first-time guest return again and again. Through this engaging, story-driven approach, you'll discover how to develop and implement changes that lead to repeat visits and, eventually, to sustained growth in your church or ministry.